BOOK OF

School
Jokes

Designed and illustrated by Leonard Le Rolland

Edited by Laura Howell

Additional research by Alastair Smith

Managing designer: Ruth Russell

CONTENTS

School Daze

Our class is like a zoo!

What do you call an ant who hates school?

A tru-ant.

What did the rabbit say to the school librarian?

"Can I burrow this book?"

What do you get when you cross a teacher with a grizzly bear?

I don't know, but when it gives a lesson, you'd better pay attention.

Why was the chicken sent home from school?

For using fowl language.

Why did the chicken get detention?

She was always playing practical yolks.

I'm sick (of school)

Nurse, I can't stop clucking, and it frightens me.

Oh, don't be such a chicken.

Nurse, I'm in the school band and I swallowed my harmonica. What should I do?

Be thankful you don't play the piano.

Nurse, I think I've turned into a cookie.

Yes, you do look a bit crumby.

Nurse, I've got lettuce sticking out of my ear.

Oh dear. I fear that it may be just the tip of the iceberg.

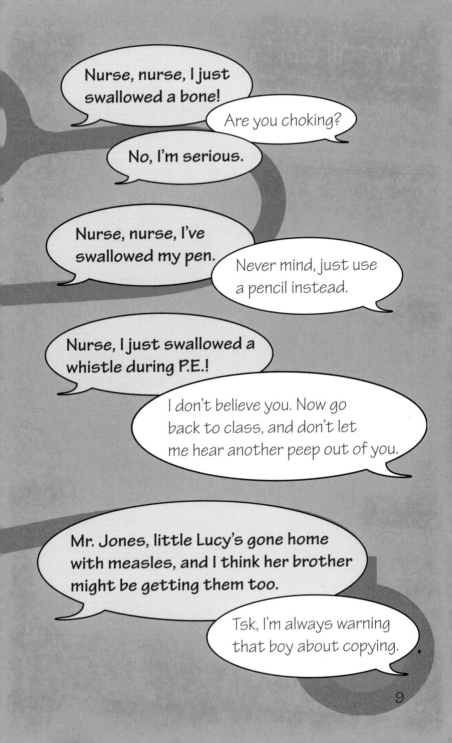

9

I'm still sick!

Nurse: Billy, you're always coming to see me. What's wrong with you this time?

Billy: I sprained my ankle running down the hall.

Nurse: That's a lame excuse.

Kid: Nurse, I feel like I'm turning into a pancake.

Nurse: Oh, how waffle.

Kid: I had trouble with diarrhoea at school today.

Mother: That's terrible! I didn't know you were ill.

Kid: I wasn't, I just couldn't spell it.

Kid: Nurse, I keep thinking I'm the school bell.

Nurse: Take these tablets, and if they don't help, give me a ring in the morning.

Kid: Nurse, are you absolutely sure this cream will cure my terrible acne?

Nurse: Of course, I never make rash promises.

Kid: **Nurse, I keep thinking I'm a headlouse.**

Nurse: I wish you'd get out of my hair.

Kid: **Nurse, I just can't stop stealing from the other kids.**

Nurse: Hmm, have you taken anything for it?

Kid: **Nurse, the other kids tease me. They say I smell like a fish.**

Nurse: You poor sole.

Why did the class joker go to the hospital?

To learn some sick jokes.

Nurse: How did you get that black eye?

Kid: You see that tree outside?

Nurse: Yes...

Kid: Well, I didn't.

Careers day

Kid: I want to be a policeman and climb trees all day, like my dad.

Careers advisor: Policemen don't climb trees, dear.

Kid: My dad does, he told me he works for the special branch.

Careers advisor: Do you have a career in mind?

Kid: I think I'd make a good book keeper.

Careers advisor: Why's that?

Kid: Well, I've had some library books since my first day at school.

Careers advisor: Tell me, what would you like to be when you grow up?

Kid: I want to be a lumberjack.

Careers advisor: Hmm, do you really think you can hack it?

Kid: Do you think I'd make a good plumber?

Careers advisor: Maybe, but you might find the work too draining.

Kid: When I leave school, I'd like to be a baker. I hear they make lots of dough.

Careers advisor: Well, you're certainly good at loafing around.

Careers advisor: What does your dad do for a living, Bobby?

Bobby: He sits around and makes faces all day.

Careers advisor: How unusual. Is he some kind of entertainer?

Bobby: No, he works in a clock factory.

Careers advisor: I see. And what does your mother do?

Bobby: She shoots people and blows them up.

Careers advisor: Don't be silly!

Bobby: It's true, she's a photographer.

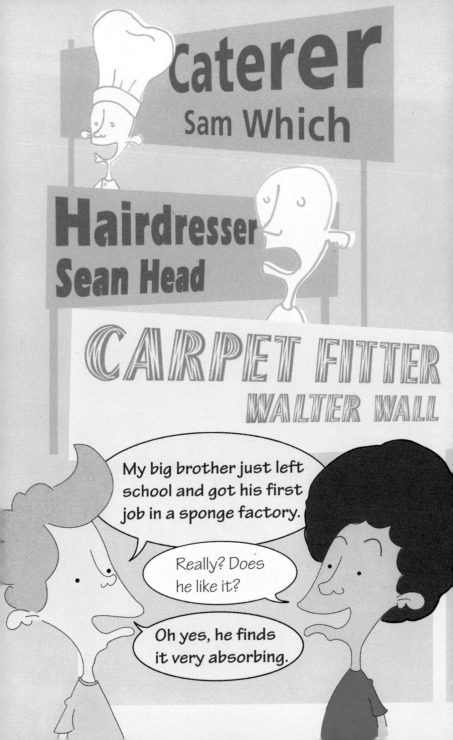

www (world wide wackiness)

Kid: Sorry I'm late. I dreamed I was surfing the Web.
Teacher: How could that make you late for school?
Kid: I had to go back to sleep to switch off the computer.

How does the class joker send messages?
By tee-hee mail.

Kid: I went to this Web site to find out what a citrus fruit is, but it won't work.
Teacher: Hmm, perhaps the lime is busy.

Who has the best Web site in the animal world?
The Onlion King.

Teacher: I'm a bit worried about letting you repair my expensive new laptop.
Computer teacher: Don't worry, of all the computers I've ever repaired, only one has ever blown up.
Teacher: How many computers have you repaired?
Computer teacher: This will be my second.

Mandy: What should you do if you get lots of e-mails saying "What's up, Doc? What's up, Doc?"
Andy: Check for bugs in your system.

Peter: I use the Internet to tell me what the weather's like.
Anita: How do you do that?
Peter: I carry my laptop outside and if it gets wet, I know it's raining.

Kid: Would you mind e-mailing my test results to my parents?
Teacher: But your parents don't have a computer.
Kid: Exactly!

Why were the kids in computer class scratching their heads?
They had internits.

School Library

Birdwatching — Jack Daw

Diary of a Bank Robber — HANS UPP

WHEN DOES SCHOOL END? — WENDY BELLGOES

SPORTS DAY — Willy Win, illustrated by Betty Wont

Healthy Breakfast Foods — Lena Bacon

Adding for Beginners — Juan & Juan Mextoo

Getting into Trouble — Kermit Crimes

A Week Off School — Trudi Light

HELP WITH YOUR HOMEWORK — Linda Hand

Finding a Penpal — Miles Apart

THE BIG BANG — Dinah Mite

The Story of the Titanic — Mandy Lifeboats

Tree Felling — Tim Burr

Noise in the Classroom — Constance Snoring

Never Give Up

Art Class

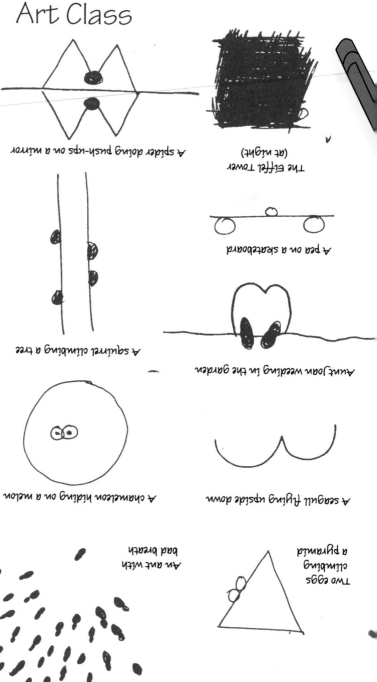

A spider doing push-ups on a mirror

The Eiffel Tower
(at night)

A squirrel climbing a tree

A pea on a skateboard

Aunt Joan weeding in the garden

A chameleon hiding on a melon

A seagull flying upside down

Two eggs
climbing
a pyramid

An ant with
bad breath

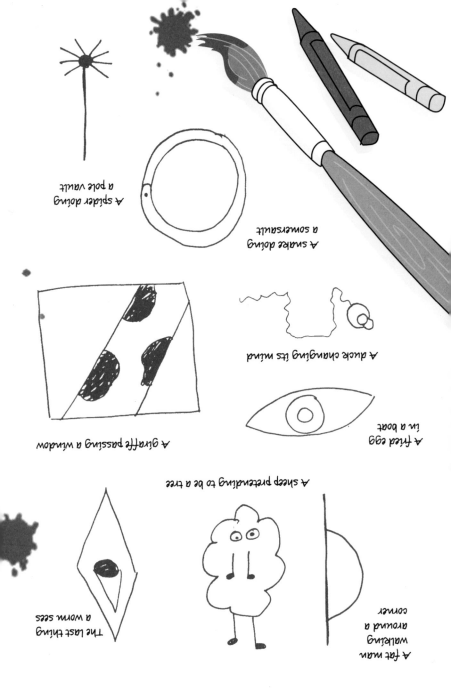

A spider doing
a pole vault

A snake doing
a somersault

A duck changing its mind

A fried egg
in a boat

A giraffe passing a window

A sheep pretending to be a tree

The last thing
a worm sees

A fat man
walking
around a
corner

21

Food, glorious food

Mother: Why have you been sent home from school early?

Kid: I set fire to something in cookery class.

Mother: That's a bit careless. What was it?

Kid: School.

Drew: Can you tell me what's in this cake you made?

Lou: Why, are you going to try making one?

Drew: No, my doctor might need to know.

Cookery teacher: Jenny, what are the best things to put in a fruit cake?

Jenny: Your teeth.

Jane: My cookery teacher didn't like what I made in class today.

Wayne: What did you make? A pie? A pizza?

Jane: A big mess.

What do the parents of the richest kid in school make for dinner every night?

Reservations.

Peter: I always know when dinner's ready in our house.

Rita: Why, do your parents call you?

Peter: No, the smoke alarm goes off.

Barry: How do you think they keep flies out of the school cafeteria?

Gary: Maybe they let them taste the food.

Teacher: Stop this food fight at once! Do you have any idea what goes into preparing your school meals?

Kid: Yes, that's why we started throwing them instead of eating them.

Teacher: What started that food fight in the cafeteria?

Kid: The bread rolls, Mr. Lee. Next came the cheese pie, and finally dessert.

It's a
dirty job...

Teacher: Why are you wearing two jackets?

Caretaker: Because I'm about to paint the hallway and it says on the tin that two coats are best.

Caretaker: Can I play on the school soccer team next season?

Soccer coach: Yes, I think you'd make a good sweeper.

Teacher 1: Do you find the new caretaker a little unfriendly?

Teacher 2: Yes, I tried talking to him the other day and he gave me the brush-off.

Teacher: My goodness, you sound terrible. You really should take something for that cold.

Caretaker: Good idea. I'll take the rest of the week off!

What do you call a pair of caretakers?

Partners in grime.

Caretaker: I quit!

Teacher: Why? What's the matter?

Caretaker: Nothing really, it's just time I made a clean sweep of things.

Did you hear? Miss White ran off with the caretaker.

Really?

Yeah, I heard he swept her off her feet.

I once had a classmate named Britt,
Who thought that he was quite a wit.
When I disagreed,
He said "Well, you need
A funnybone transplant, you twit!"

Ever wondered how comedians learn to be funny? They go to Joke School, where making your teacher laugh is the only rule!

Teacher: OK class, can anybody tell me what is yellow, has big teeth and lives in a fruit bowl?

Pupil: Sorry, no idea.

Teacher: A banana. I lied about the teeth.

Teacher: What's the definition of a snail?

Pupil: It's a little slimy animal with a hard shell.

Teacher: Wrong, wrong, wrong! It's a slug wearing a crash helmet.

Teacher: Why do doctors' bags snore?

Pupil: But that's silly. They don't snore, they're bags!

Teacher: Yes they do... because they're full of sleeping pills.

Teacher: Can anyone give me a definition of politics?

Pupil: It's the name given to the complex relationships between those in power and the people they govern.

Teacher: Wrong! It's what happens to your pet parrot if he swallows a clock.

Teacher: Class, do you know why tall people have long arms?

Pupil: Because if they were short they'd be out of proportion with the rest of their bodies?

Teacher: Nonsense! It's because if their arms were shorter they wouldn't reach their hands.

Teacher: What's green and scaly and goes "Hith, hith?"

Pupil: I give up.

Teacher: It's a snake with a lisp, of course!

Teacher: What's a clamera?

Pupil: Don't you mean camera?

Teacher: No, a clamera is what you get if you cross a shellfish with a picture-taking device.

Teacher: What goes moo, baa, oink, woof, quack?

Pupil: I don't know.

Teacher: Come on, at least try to be funny. It's a cow that can speak five languages.

Teacher: Why do elephants have wrinkled feet?

Pupil: Er, because their shoes are too tight?

Teacher: Correct! Now you're getting the hang of things.

Teacher: What did the baboon say when it swallowed a stick of dynamite?

Pupil: Ba-boom!

Teacher: Yes! You are an excellent student.

Teacher: How do you know if there's an elephant in your refrigerator?

Pupil: Ooh, I think I know this one – your nose touches the ceiling?

Teacher: Good try, but wrong punchline. The answer is, you find footprints in the butter.

Teacher: How do you keep a skunk from smelling?

Pupil: Remove his scent glands.

Teacher: Wrong! You hold his nose.

Teacher: What did the bird say when it laid a square egg?

Pupil: There's no such thing as a square egg, is there?

Teacher: You are a terrible student! The answer is simply "Ouch!"

Teacher: What kind of bus crossed the ocean?

Pupil: Sir, a bus is a land vehicle. It couldn't cross the...

Teacher: No, no, no! The answer is Colum-bus!

Teacher: What kind of key opens a banana?

Pupil: That's a trick question. You don't need a key to open a banana.

Teacher: Wrong. The answer is a monkey.

Teacher: You, boy. What kind of lights do you think Noah used on his ark?

Smart kid: I believe oil lamps were commonly used in that era, sir.

Teacher: That may be correct, but it doesn't make me laugh. He used floodlights.

Teacher: What is the hardest thing to eat?

Pupil: Er, a rock cake?

Teacher: No, a banana.

Pupil: Bananas aren't hard to eat...

Teacher: Clearly you've never tried to eat one sideways.

Teacher: Tell me, what do you call a pig with three eyes?

Pupil: Some kind of horrible mutant?

Teacher: Not at all. It's a piiig.

Teacher: Does anyone know what is orange and sounds like a parrot?

Pupil: Erm, some kind of canary or bird of paradise?

Teacher: Not even close. The answer is a carrot.

Teacher: How does one recognize a dogwood tree?

Pupil: By its small size and attractive white blossoms.

Teacher: Probably true, but not very amusing. The answer is, you listen to its bark.

Teacher: What do we know about a bird in the hand, class?

Pupil: That it's worth two in the bush?

Teacher: Well, I'd say it makes it hard to blow your nose.

33

Teacher: Why is a pea small and green?

Pupil: Because it contains chlorophyll.

Teacher: No, because if it were big and yellow, you might mistake it for the school bus.

Teacher: How do you fit an elephant into a matchbox?

Pupil: Erm, I don't know.

Teacher: Take out the matches, obviously! Now let's try that again. How do you fit a hippo into a matchbox?

Pupil: Take out the matches?

Teacher: No, take out the elephant!

Teacher: Why do hummingbirds hum?

Pupil: It's the noise their wings make as they beat them.

Teacher: Don't be ridiculous. It's because they don't know the words.

Teacher: Tell me, if frozen tea is iced tea, what is frozen ink?

Pupil: Iced ink.

Teacher: Well, take a bath then!

Teacher: What kind of animal has four legs and can see just as well at both ends?

Pupil: Surely some kind of mythical beast?

Teacher: Really? What about a horse with its eyes closed?

Teacher: Why do you think a stork lifts one leg?

Pupil: Some kind of evolutionary quirk?

Teacher: Don't try to be too clever. If it lifted both legs, it would fall over.

Can anyone answer this: when is a car not a car?

When it's become scrap metal?

Not bad, but the answer is when it turns into a side street.

Teacher: Today's lesson is about riddles. What flies but never goes anywhere?

Pupil: Um... a lost homing pigeon?

Teacher: Good try, but the answer is a flag.

Teacher: What is a kitten after it's fourteen days old?

Pupil: A young cat?

Teacher: No, no. It's fifteen days old.

Teacher: What has fifty legs, but can't walk?

Pupil: Let me think... half a centipede?

Teacher: Not bad, but the answer is twelve and a half tables.

Teacher: What kind of room can you never enter?

Pupil: I'd say a room without a door.

Teacher: Good guess, but no. It's a mushroom.

Teacher: Tell me, boy. What is red and invisible?

Pupil: I don't know, I can't see it.

Teacher: Try harder. The answer is no tomatoes.

Teacher: Can you name something that is full of holes, yet can still hold water?

Pupil: But if something has holes, the water would leak out.

Teacher: Haven't you ever seen a sponge?

Teacher: What goes "Oom, Oom"?

Pupil: Some kind of siren?

Teacher: Ridiculous! It's a cow walking backwards.

Teacher: Tell me, what do you think would happen if you threw a blue stone in the Red Sea?

Pupil: Well, red and blue make purple. So would it turn purple?

Teacher: Of course not. It would just get wet.

Teacher: What pet do you think makes the loudest noise?

Pupil: Hmm... perhaps a parrot or a big dog?

Teacher: Think more carefully. It's a trumpet.

Teacher: What is black and white and red all over?

Pupil: A penguin with sunburn!

Teacher: Well done! I also would have accepted an embarrassed panda or a nun with a nosebleed.

Teacher: What would happen if you were to cross a dog with a plant?

Smart kid: I'm sure modern genetic technology wouldn't allow such a thing.

Teacher: What? Haven't you ever seen a field full of collieflowers?

Teacher: Class, what has four legs and flies?

Pupil: I've heard this one. It's two pairs of jeans.

Teacher: Don't be silly. It's a dead cow.

Teacher: Think carefully. What is green and square?

Pupil: Let's see... a football field? A pool table?

Teacher: Wrong. It's an orange in disguise.

Teacher: What's the difference between a piano, a fish and a tube of glue?

Pupil: Don't know.

Teacher: You can tune a piano, but you can't tuna fish. Get it?

Pupil: But what about the glue?

Teacher: Ah, I thought that's where you'd get stuck.

I must say, you're the most well-behaved and academically-minded pupils I've taught in a long time.

Thank you, teacher!

I'm very disappointed in you all. Stay behind after school and write "I must fool around more in class" on the board one million times.

But – !

Only joking.

The Great Outdoors

Further afield

The school went on a field trip to the Natural History Museum in London. "How was it?" asked Jimmy's mother when he returned.

"It was the worst zoo I've ever been to," he replied. "All the animals were dead!"

Pupil: Mr. Smith, what's big and red, and has ten legs and fangs?

Teacher: I've no idea, why do you ask?

Pupil: Because one just crawled up your trouser leg.

Mother: Did you enjoy the field trip today, dear?

Kid: Oh yes. In fact, we're going back tomorrow.

Mother: Really, why?

Kid: To try and find the kids we left behind.

Teacher: I'm thinking of taking my class to the zoo tomorrow.

Teacher 2: I wouldn't bother. If the zoo wants them, they can come and collect them.

Teacher: Tom, we carry whistles on a hike in case of an emergency. Don't blow yours all the time.

Tom: But I'm using it to scare away tigers, Mr. Lee.

Teacher: There are no tigers here.

Tom: That proves how well the whistle works.

Teacher 1: Why do you dread taking your pupils overseas?

Teacher 2: Because every time they get on a ferry, it makes them cross.

Wendy: That cow over there is a pretty shade of brown, Miss White.

Teacher: Yes, Wendy. It's a Jersey.

Wendy: Really? I didn't know cows wore jerseys...

Fun and games

Soccer coach: Why didn't you stop the ball?
Kid: That's what the net's for, isn't it?

Sunita: My brother wanted to enter a marathon, but he decided to go to college first.
Rita: Why was that?
Sunita: Our parents always told us that education pays off in the long run.

Kid: Coach, the soccer field's flooded. What should we do?
Coach: Bring on the subs.

Teacher: Jane, write out "I must not forget my P.E. kit" 100 times.
Jane: But Mr. Jenkins, I only forgot it once.

Barry: What's the difference between the school soccer team's goalkeeper and Cinderella?
Carrie: Cinderella got to the ball.

Why are you swimming on your back?

You told us never to swim on a full stomach.

Joan: Why are the kids from art class no good in sports matches?

Jane: They keep drawing.

Katie: Why don't you play football with Martin any more?

Kevin: Would you play with someone who cheats and kicks people all the time?

Katie: No...

Kevin: Well, neither would he.

Teacher: Who was the fastest runner in history?

Kid: Adam, because he came first in the human race.

Johnny: I can't believe I just missed that goal. I could kick myself.

Jimmy: Don't bother, you'd probably miss.

Billy: My P.E. teacher wouldn't listen to me when I said I was no good at throwing the javelin.

Lily: What happened?

Billy: Oh, he got the point eventually.

P.E. teacher: Hey! Don't dive into that swimming pool, there's no water in it!

Kid: It's OK, I can't swim.

Benny: What has eleven heads and runs around screaming?

Lenny: The school hockey team.

P.E. teacher: It is a well-known fact that exercise kills germs.

Kid: But how do you get the germs to exercise?

P.E. teacher: Why won't you attempt the high jump?

Kid: I'm scared of heights.

P.E. teacher: Well, try the long jump then.

Kid: I can't do that, I'm short-sighted.

Kid: I don't think I made the school shot putt team.

Dad: Why not?

Kid: The coach said I was so bad, I couldn't throw myself to the floor.

Molly: Who's the best-looking boy in school?

Holly: The leader of the running team, because he's always dashing.

Meanwhile, on the playground...

Ricky: I'm having a bad day, all my teachers are criticizing me.

Lucy: Really?

Ricky: Yeah, in fact, my art teacher just said I'm so talentless, I couldn't draw breath.

Karen: It's true there's a link between television and bad language.

Darren: How do you know?

Karen: I told my teacher I'd watched TV instead of doing my homework, and she yelled at me.

Gary: Do you want to walk back home through the spooky graveyard tonight?

Barry: No way, I wouldn't be seen dead there.

Are you trying to make a fool out of me?

No, I never like to interfere with nature.

Andy: My teacher's a peach.

Mandy: You mean she's sweet?

Andy: No, I mean she has a heart of stone.

What do you call a teacher with chalk in his ears?

Anything you like, he can't hear you.

What do you think you're doing, telling everyone I'm stupid?

Sorry, I didn't know it was supposed to be a secret.

Jez: What kind of car does your dad have?

Les: I can't remember, but I think it starts with t.

Jez: Really? My dad's starts with fuel.

What's the difference between an ice cream and the meanest kid in school?

You lick one, the other licks you.

You two boys! Stop fighting at once. You should learn to give and take.

We did. He took my sandwich and I gave him a slap.

Gina: The toughest kid in school threatened to hit me if I didn't give him my lunch.

Sabrina: That's awful!

Gina: You don't know my mother's cooking. He offered to do my homework if I took it back.

Big kid: I'm gonna mop the floor with your face, kid.

Little kid: Hah, you'll be sorry.

Big kid: Oh yeah, why's that?

Little kid: You won't be able to get into the corners very well.

Teacher: If you had ten chocolates, and the boy next to you took away seven, what would you have?

Kid: A big fight, Mr. Lee.

Teacher: Why are you crying, Sophie?

Sophie: Anna broke my new ruler.

Teacher: How did she do that?

Sophie: I hit her with it.

Teacher: Who broke this window?

Carl: It was Lenny, Miss Smith.
I threw an apple at him and he moved away.

You've been fighting again, haven't you? Look, you've lost your two front teeth.

No I haven't, Mr. Lee.
They're in my pocket.

A teacher whose temper was short,
Would shout, when a pupil was caught
With no homework to show,
"To the corner you'll go,
Where you'll stay 'til you do
as you're taught!"

Test stress

I hope I didn't see you looking at Anna's exam paper.

I hope you didn't see me, too.

I don't think I deserve zero for this test, Mr. Lee.

Nor do I, but it's the lowest grade I'm allowed to give you.

I'm taking exams in French, Spanish and algebra this year.

If you're so clever, let's hear you say "Hello" in Algebra.

Why shouldn't you put gel on your hair the day before an exam?

If you did, all the answers might slip your mind.

Les: Great news, teacher says we'll have a test today come rain or shine.

Jez: What's so great about that?

Les: It's snowing outside!

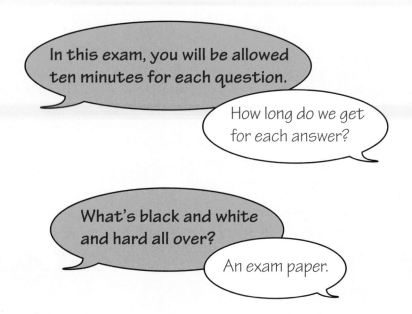

In this exam, you will be allowed ten minutes for each question.

How long do we get for each answer?

What's black and white and hard all over?

An exam paper.

Why did the skeleton schoolgirl stay late at school?

She was boning up for her exams.

Dad: Were your exam results good?

Kid: Yes and no.

Dad: What do you mean, "yes and no"?

Kid: Yes, my exam results were no good.

Dad: Why did you get such a low score in that exam?

Kid: Absence.

Dad: You were absent on the day of the exam?

Kid: No, but the boy who sits next to me was.

> How did you do in your exams?

> I failed everything except history.

> How did you manage that?

> I didn't take history.

What do you get if you cross a vampire and a teacher?

Lots of blood tests.

Mother: How were the exam questions?

Kid: Easy.

Mother: Why do you look so miserable, then?

Kid: The questions didn't give me any trouble, but the answers were really hard.

General knowledge

1. What important discovery led Archimedes to leap out of his bathtub and shout "Eureka!"?

That the water was too hot.

2. Where are the largest animals found?

In the sea because they won't fit anywhere else.

3. Name a bird of prey.

The priest's pet canary.

4. If a person from Rome is called a Roman, what is a person from Paris called?

A parasite.

....

History

5. What did Napoleon become on his 30th birthday?

A year older.

6. Where was America's Declaration of Independence signed?

At the bottom.

English

7. What is the most important thing to remember about grammar?

She's a bit deaf so you need to speak loudly to her.

8. What should you do with double negatives?

Don't never use them.

....

Physics

9. Describe the process of conduction.

The way the sound of music spreads from one place to another.

Chemistry

10. Name a type of hard water.

Ice

11. Describe the periodic table.

An item of furniture that you don't use all the time.

Human biology

12. What does a blood vessel do?

Carries Count Dracula across the sea.

13. Explain the process of respiration.

When you breathe you inspire. When you don't you expire.

14. What is a skeleton?

A person with his insides out and his outsides off.

15. What is the fibula?

A small lie.

16. When might you have an ultrasound test?

When you buy a new CD player.

17. How are genes inherited?

When my brother grows out of them.

Earth and space

18. Describe the equator.

It is an imaginary lion running all around the Earth through Africa.

19. Give a fact about the Sun.

Some people use the Sun to tell the time but I've never been able to see the numbers.

20. Name two things you might find on the seabed.

Sea sheets and sea pillows.

....

Science

21. Describe a magnet.

A little white thing that you might find in a rotten apple.

22. Define momentum.

Something you buy to remind yourself of a place you visited.

Ghoul School

Ghostly goings-on

What do little ghosts do their homework in?

Exorcise books.

What position did the ghost play on the school soccer team?

Ghoulkeeper.

What did the ghost teacher tell her pupils?

"Spook when you're spooken to!"

What *do* ghosts play in the school band?

Haunting melodies.

How *do* they learn to play them?

They study the sheet music.

Ghost kid: My hamster ate my homework.

Ghost teacher: Don't try your lame excuses on me. I can see right through you.

Did you hear about the ghosts who went to the school dance?

They had a wail of a time.

Where do ghosts get an education?

High sghoul.

65

I'm having a funny spell...

What is a little witch's best subject in school?

Spell-ing.

**How did the little witch know
when it was time to go to school?**

She looked at her witchwatch.

**Why was the teacher confused when he had
to teach a pair of witch twins?**

He couldn't tell which witch was which.

What did it say on the witch's report card?

Her work is good, but there's broom for improvement.

Why did the witch teachers go on strike?

They wanted sweeping reforms.

How do you know if you're sitting next to a witch in class?

She has a big "W" on her pencilcase.

Kid 1: Are you having a birthday party this year?

Kid 2: No, I'm having a witch do.

Kid 1: What's a witch do?

Kid 2: She flies around on a broomstick, of course.

What was the name of the little witch's father?

He was cauld-ron.

67

Rib-tickling skeleton jokes

What instrument did the little skeleton play in the school band?

The trom-bone.

What do you call a skeleton who's late for school every morning?

Lazy bones.

Why didn't you go to the school dance?

I had no body to go with.

What happened when the ghost teachers went on strike?

They were replaced by a skeleton staff.

Sghoul dinner menu

Starters

Tomb-ato soup
Dread rolls

Main courses

Spookghetti
Monster mash with grave-y
Ghoul-ash
Devilled eggs
Baked beings
Fried lice
Toads in the hole

Desserts

Ice scream
Booberry pie
Blood oranges
Leeches and cream

There was a young werewolf named Mary,
Whose body was terribly hairy.
Her classmates would scoff,
"If you shaved it all off,
we'd still think you're ugly and scary!"

LITTLE
MONSTERS

Simply monstrous

Why are little monsters so good at adding?

They can count up to 25 on their fingers.

What's the difference between a nice teacher and the Loch Ness Monster?

There's a chance the Loch Ness Monster might exist.

How do monsters like their eggs served in the school cafeteria?

Terror-fried.

What game do monsters like best?

Swallow my leader.

Why was the monster teacher getting angry?
Everything he told his class went in one ear and out the others.

Why was the two-headed monster bad at geography?
Because he never knew if he was coming or going.

Teacher: What would you do if you saw a huge, green monster?
Kid: Hope it hadn't seen me first.

Why did the one-eyed monster give up teaching?
He only had one pupil.

Did you hear about the monster teachers who got married?
It was love at first fright.

Why did the yeti go to the school nurse?

He was feeling abominable.

How does Quasimodo bring his sandwiches to school?

In the lunch pack of Notre Dame.

Why did the school cook shout at the troll?

She saw him goblin his food.

Kid: Dad, the other kids are mean to me. They call me a werewolf.

Dad: Be quiet and comb your face.

Why did the little werewolf get asked so many questions in class?

Because she always gave snappy answers.

Did you hear about the cannibal who was expelled from school?

He was buttering up his teacher.

How do you spot a cannibal kid in the school cafeteria?

He asks for the cook.

Why was Frankenstein's monster best friends with the class joker?

She always kept him in stitches.

Why did the two cyclops children fight?

They couldn't see eye to eye over anything.

Vampires

What happened to the vampires on sports day?

They finished the race neck and neck.

What do vampires learn in school?

The alpha-bat.

Did you hear about the vampire who was in the school play?

He had a bit part.

What do polite vampire children say?

Fang you very much.

What school meal do vampires hate most?

Stake and fries.

Why did the little vampire go to the school nurse?

He was always coffin.

What after-school club do vampire children join?

A blood group.

Why did the little vampire join art class?

He was good at drawing blood.

Die laughing

Why did the little vampire have no friends in school?

Because he was a pain in the neck.

What was the little vampire's idea of fast food?

Someone with high blood pressure.

What did the little vampire have with his apple pie in the school cafeteria?

Vein-illa ice cream.

Teacher, I studied really hard. Did I pass my test?

I'm sorry, Vlad. All your efforts were in vein.

Why do demons and ghouls sit together in class?

Because demons are a ghoul's best friend.

Why was the zombie school so popular?

Kids were dying to get into it.

Why do zombies study Latin and Ancient Greek?

Because they like dead languages.

Who did the zombie take to the junior prom?

Any old girl he could dig up.

My literature teacher, Miss Mann,
Wrote poems that never would scan.
When asked "Why's that so?"
She said "I don't know,
But maybe it's because I always try to
cram as many words into the last line
as I possibly can!"

Dikshunry

The book that helps you write
"right" or "write" right

A

Abundance A dance which is held in a bakery.

Accidents Emergency teeth to temporarily replace those knocked out by mistake.

Acorn Something painful on my dad's toe.

Acrobat Kind of flying creature that shows off a lot.

Adverse A poem that seems to get longer the more you read it.

Afford Popular type of car.

Antelope Event involving two bugs who fall in love and run away together.

Apex A gorilla's old girlfriend.

Arrest Something you take when you are tired.

Atom Male cat.

Automate Robot's best friend.

B

Backgammon Game that pigs play.

Barbarian A hairdresser called Ian.

Beehive An order given by bees to their misbehaving children.

Belly dancer A ballet dancer, spelled badly.

Berets What French people put in fruit pies.

Blazer A jacket that is on fire.

Blood brother Dracula's closest relative.

Bombastic A long, thin explosive, like dynamite.

Bonus What dogs gnawed in ancient Rome.

Bulldozer A male cow, asleep.

Butterfly Genetic experiment involving a bird and a goat.

C

Cabbage A taxi's age.

Camelot A herd of north African humped animals.

Carnation A country where everyone owns a car.

Carpet A dog that sits in its owner's vehicle all day.

Castanets What Spanish fishermen do when they go fishing.

Chilli powder Very fine snowflakes.

Chinchilla Special device for cooling the lower jaw.

Circumference The knight who invented the round table.

Cocktail Drink made from a rooster's rear end.

Commentator A talking spud.

D

Dark Ages Knight time!

Deadline Perimeter of a cemetery.

Decide You'll find this just around from defront.

Denial Big river in Egypt.

Disband When members of a rock group fall out with one another.

Dogmatic Kind of robot dog.

Dogma A puppy's mother.

Doing The noise a spring makes.

Donation A country full of female deer.

Dramatic That terrible business you have to go through to get that wretched parasite off your dog's back.

Barney -tic

E

Earwig False hair that comes down over the ears.

Eclipse What a male gardener does to a hedge.

Elastic band An old rock group that keeps bouncing back.

Elderberry Wisest fruit on the branch.

Electric eel Fish that thrives in strong currents.

Electroplate What atomic scientists eat their dinner from.

Emulate What people do when they copy the movements of a very large Australian bird.

Encumber The watery bit in the middle of a cucumber.

Exhale Like frozen rain, except that it's now turned slushy.

Explosion Result of experiment.

F

Fan belt What a soccer fan uses to keep trousers up.

Father-in-law Dad, in jail.

Fiction What a teacher thinks of your homework excuses.

Fiddlesticks Violin bows.

Finale Good quality French beer.

Fish fingers Things that marine animals point at each other.

Fjord Norwegian car.

Flamenco A big, pink, dancing bird.

Flattery A worn-out electricity source.

Flea market Where dogs go to get their next infestation.

Flippant A small, industrious bug on its back.

Flypaper What spiders decorate their homes with.

G

Galleon A unit of measurement used on very old ships.

Gamekeeper A soccer goalie who doesn't get upset, despite losing heavily.

Gangrene To be feeling sick.

Gateau French for "Fetch water".

Genius A very intelligent person who lives in a magic lamp.

Geranium A nuclear fuel that smells nice.

Gigantic The biggest, scariest bug in your dog's fur.

Glossary Paint store.

Goblet A genetically modified, small turkey.

gobble gobble

Grammar Grandad's wife.

Granivore A monster that devours grandmothers.

H

Halo A word that angels use to greet each other.

Hamlet Small piece of pork.

Handicap Useful headgear.

Hasty Quick snack that stimulates the tongue.

Hatchet What a hen does to its egg.

Hogwash Pig's laundry.

Holy What my old socks are.

Honesty A fear of being caught.

Honeycomb Hair styling tool used by bees.

Hornet What a goat does with its head to something that it doesn't like.

Housefly A small insect with wings, six legs and a roof.

Humbug Musical insect.

I

Ice cream What I do when scared.

Idolize Lazy eyeballs.

Ignoramus A big, stupid animal that wallows in mud.

Illegal Bird of prey with ailment.

Impeccable Hidden from birds.

Independent Something, e.g. a picture, enclosed in a locket worn around the neck.

Infamy To feel persecuted, e.g. "They've all got it infamy!"

Information How planes fly at an air show.

Inkling A very small pen.

Intense Where you sleep while camping.

Isopod Hi-tech igloo.

J

Jailbait Prison food.

Jape You little monkey!

Jargon Fancy word for the loss of a glass receptacle.

Jeans What chromosomes wear.

Je ne sais quoi Sorry, I don't know what this means...

Jitterbug Insect that's had too much coffee.

Joan of Arc Noah's wife.

Joint account Money saved up to buy meat.

Jubilant Triumphant insect.

Juggernaut Jug full of nothing.

Jumbo Flying elephant.

Justice What's left in the glass after you've drunk the lemonade.

Juvenile Small African river before it got huge.

K

Karate A drink enjoyed by martial artists.

Keratin What preserved carrots are sold in.

Ketchup Command shouted at tomato that is slowest to ripen.

Kettle drum What musicians boil water in.

Khaki What soldiers use to make their vehicles start.

Kidnap Something that a young child takes when tired.

Kidney That thing halfway down a kid's leg.

Kindred Fear of being visited by relatives.

Kinetics Science of understanding your family.

Kinship The family's boat.

Kipper Fish that likes to sleep.

L

Landmark Imprint made by unsuccessful skydiver.

Lassitude A heroic dog with attitude.

Launch Midday meal for astronauts.

Launch pad To throw a notebook at a classmate.

Lavish Resembling a lavatory.

Lazy bones An idle person's skeleton.

Legend The foot.

Light sleeper Someone who falls asleep with the light on.

Locomotive A crazy reason for doing something.

Logarithms Tunes played at a lumberjack's birthday party.

Lollypop Dad's money.

M

Macro Scottish bird.

Malady The correct way to address a female aristocrat.

Mammoth Giant flying bug thing.

Marigold To become the wife or husband of somebody who is very, very rich.

Maritime Wedding day at the seaside.

Market What teachers do to homework.

Melancholy Dog that likes watery fruit.

Milk shake Drink given by nervous cows.

Mothball What moths play football with.

Mug Gullible drinks receptacle.

Mutant Genetically altered ant.

N

Naturalist Carefully compiled information about plants and animals.

Navvy Misspelling of a bunch of people going around in boats.

Newfangled Grandpa shows off his latest set of dentures.

Nightingale To spend a night outside in the wind.

Night school Academy where Dracula and the wolfman went to study.

Nipper Baby crab.

Nitty-gritty How a dirty scalp looks, up close.

Noisette Small, crunching sound a nut makes when it is cracked.

Norm Just a regular kinda guy.

Novelty Unusual-tasting herbal beverage.

O

Observant What a biology teacher tells you to do when out looking for bugs.

Occidental Something unplanned that happened in the Far East.

Octopus Strange, genetically modified, eight-legged cat.

Offal Something dreadful.

Offence Aggressive-looking boundary around your house.

Operatics Bugs that live in an opera house.

Operetta Person who gives tuneful advice if you have trouble using your phone.

Opportune Music played by entertainer on a pogo stick.

Optical When your eyes itch.

Otter What water becomes as you heat it.

P

Palate What a cannibal did to his friend.

Pantry Room where you keep your trousers.

Pants Something a dog does and a man steps into.

Paradise Two perfect little cubes with dots on them.

Particle When your dad amuses you.

Password To hand a note to someone in class.

Pasteurize Too far away to see.

Pen pals Pigs that get along well.

Pickle Cucumber in trouble.

Pigswill How a dead pig leaves things to his family.

Propaganda Polite, well behaved male goose.

Q

Quack A duck's doctor.

Quadrant Four-sided insect.

Quake Fearful duck call.

Quality A very fine, hot beverage, especially drunk by the English.

Qualm Feeling odd about a coming storm.

Quarantine When a youth locks himself in his bedroom for months at a time.

Quay Something you need to start a motor boat.

Quicksand Beach where motor races are held.

Quickset Type of glue.

Quince Five children born at the same time.

Quota Someone who likes to report other people's speech.

R

Rabble A pile of debris left behind by a disorderly crowd.

Race The things that come out from the Sun and travel across space at an amazing speed.

Radiant A mutant bug which begins to glow after it's been exposed to atomic energy.

Raisin A very old-looking grape.

Ramification To make someone feel sheepish.

Rawhide A nudist's clothes.

Rebate Fishing term: to place another worm on the hook.

Rectify When you try to fix something, but end up wrecking it instead.

Rote Wot I dun in my eksersize buk.

Runner beans Food for athletes.

S

Sage A wise old herb.

Sand bank Where camels keep their money.

Scales Part of fish that weighs the most.

Sedate What you learn when you look at a calendar.

Shamrock A fake stone.

Sheepish Person who has the wool pulled over their eyes.

Sibling A baby sib.

Sleeping bag A nap sack.

Sourpuss Result of science experiment involving a cat and a lemon.

Square root Diced turnip.

Stabilized A horse that's been locked in.

Steel wool A robbery at a sheep farm.

T

Taciturn A very quiet vase.

Tangent A man who has been in the sun.

Telepathy Being too lazy to give your friends a call.

Thaw How your thumb feelth if you thtick a pin in it.

Thesaurus A talking dinosaur that uses big words.

Thoroughbred High-class baked goods.

Three-legged race Popular event at the Monster Olympic Games.

Toadstool Implement used by a toad to repair its car.

Transistor A robot's female relative.

Transparent What mothers and fathers are when hypnotized.

U

Ultramarine The best sailor in the navy.

Unabridged A river you have to swim across.

Undercover agent A spy on a camping trip.

Unflappable A word which describes a flightless bird.

Unicorn A single blemish on the foot.

Unlucky Crossing the street to avoid walking under a ladder and getting hit by a truck full of horseshoes.

Unsavoury Sweet.

Unscramble Something you can't do to an egg.

Unused A word which describes teacher's sense of humour.

Uproar What a short lion does.

V

Valid The thing on the top of a jar.

Vampire bat What Dracula uses to play baseball.

Vanish An invisible substance you paint on fences.

Varmint Troublesome candy.

Ventriloquist A man who never speaks for himself.

Veto What's on ve end of ve foot.

Victim A pair of twins in my class.

Violence Musical instruments with strings.

Viper Vhat you use to clean ze vindows.

Volcano A mountain that's blown its top.

Voltage The era that began after the discovery of electricity.

W

Waiter Someone who thinks money grows on trays.

Warehouse Where the wolfman lives.

Water polo What horses play in the swimming pool.

Water table Where fish eat their dinners.

Wattage Question you ask to find out how old someone is.

Whisker A chef who beats eggs.

Wimple A kind of blemish that nuns often develop.

X

X-ray My dead uncle Raymond.

Xylophone Revolutionary communication device that turns the sounds of the voice into a mellow, musical chime.

Y

Yawn A kind of heavy breathing used in school.

Yellow lines What you get if you misbehave at traffic school.

Yeoman A greeting you should never use for your teacher.

Yogurt Stretching exercise that makes you ache.

Youngish What your parents think they are.

Z

Zeal An enthusiastic sea mammal.

Zinc What a ship will do if it has a hole in it.

Zit Command given to a spotted dog.

Zoophyte What happens when captive gorillas annoy each other.

In summary...

Name: Mickey Mouth

Teacher's remarks:

This boy is an excellent communicator.
He never shuts up.

Name: Des Respectful

Teacher's remarks:

An independent learner.
Ignores everything I tell him.

Name: Bridget D. Fidgett

Teacher's remarks:

An active member of class.
Will not sit quietly for more than a
minute at a time.

Name: L. A. Zeebones

Teacher's remarks:

Exams do not give him any problems.
He's never turned up for one.

Name: Lynn Guist

Teacher's remarks:

Very good at using language -
the kind that earns her a detention.

Name: Wayne Payne

Teacher's remarks:

He can't wait until he leaves school. Neither can we.

Name: Lou Neetunes

Teacher's remarks:

Has an excellent ear for music. Never turns up for class without his personal stereo.

Name: S. Portsman

Teacher's remarks:

Enjoys physical activity, as it doesn't involve using his mind.

Name: Amber Dextrous

Teacher's remarks:

This pupil is excellent with her hands. She's the roughest fighter in school.

Name: R. Tistic

Teacher's remarks:

His artwork was displayed all over school, until we confiscated his spray cans.

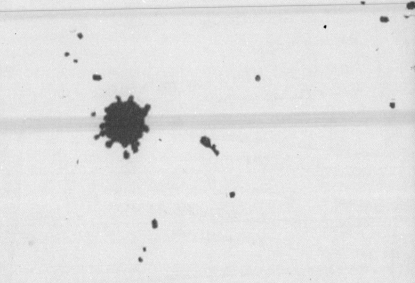

First published in 2003 by Usborne Publishing Ltd.,
Usborne House, 83-85 Saffron Hill, London, EC1N 8RT, England.
www.usborne.com

Printed in Italy

$9.95